I0117809

the artemisia

William S. Barnes

AN INLANDIA INSTITUTE PUBLICATION

INLANDIA
INSTITUTE

RIVERSIDE, CALIFORNIA

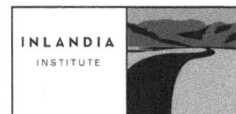

the artemisia by William S. Barnes
Copyright © 2024 William S. Barnes. All rights reserved.

ISBN: 978-1-955969-25-3

No part of this book may be used, reproduced, or adapted to public performances in any manner whatsoever without permission from both the publisher and the copyright owner, except in the case of brief quotations embodied in critical articles and reviews. For more information, write to

Permissions, Inlandia Institute, 4178 Chestnut Street, Riverside CA 92501.

Cover Art: Kaplowitz, Laurie. *Maidenhair Tree.* Acrylic, collage. Private Collection, Boston. **www.lauriekaplowitz.net, www.instagram.com/laurie.kaplowitz**

Book design and layout: Mark Givens
Printed and bound in the United States
Distributed by Ingram

Library of Congress Control Number: 2024931942

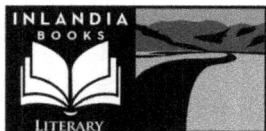

Published by Inlandia Institute
Riverside, California
www.InlandiaInstitute.org
First Edition

the artemisia

William S. Barnes

table of contents

Love has two affirmations. First of all, when the lover encounters the other, there is an immediate affirmation (psychologically: dazzlement, enthusiasm, exaltation, mad projection of a fulfilled future: I am devoured by desire, the impulse to be happy): I say *yes* to everything (blinding myself). There follows a long tunnel: my first *yes* is riddled by doubts, love's *value* is ceaselessly threatened by depreciation: this is the moment of melancholy passion, the rising of resentment and of oblation. Yet I can emerge from this tunnel; I can "surmount," without liquidating; what I have affirmed a first time, I can once again affirm, without repeating it, for then what I affirm is the affirmation, not its contingency: I affirm the first encounter in its difference, I desire its return, not its repetition. I say to the other (old or new): *Let us begin again.*

—Roland Barthes, *A Lover's Discourse*

She was the wind when wind was in my way;
Alive at noon, I perished in her form.
Who rise from flesh to spirit know the fall:
The word outleaps the world, and light is all.

—Theodore Roethke, *The Vigil*

Originally, Artemis was ruler of the stars.

—Robert Graves, *The Greek Gods*

At this point, she is all bird.

—Anne Baring & Jules Cashford, *The Myth of the Goddess*

the artemisia

> *she teaches writing at the school for girls.*
once...

we climbed the mountain alone together. into the woods.
first pine. then aspen and plum in the carved-out places. where the water gathers.

each day, she leads them outside.
to follow the sound. upward. into the story.

we swim all morning. tracing the colored stones. the shallows' edge. talking and talking.
dazzling. bright. the watery skin of it. otters, spinning! till something in the air, in the light

shifts. *these. her children. fall into the grass, the leaves.*
her chorus. her seeds.

it's like this every morning. here, before the wind. before the clouds. that pause.
we drift apart. flecks of wood. the water stills.

> *—she begins with the names of things. until the names begin to move.*
a manuscript of letters: infinitives: pinaceae, salicaceae, rosaceae.

you float in circles, at the bank by the sedges, your face to the sky.
I lie on the shore, my arms in the water, listening to you. a trail of moss.

a long, sinuous wave. *they watch her speak. they watch her lips.*
cyperaceae, poaceae, iridaceae.

to be held like that. luminous. inside. until the edges of each breath
sharpen again. *to mirror the shape of her words. the lift of her chin. her gaze.*

what had been warm and yellow, now cool and violet and cut.
primulaceae, onagraceae, campanulaceae.

I look up.
into the glare.

she sees the birds in their eyes. in her own. mallard. heron. considers the syntax
of this place. of their bodies inside it. each. to each. to water. to light.

a sudden shadow at the verge, at the bank, just above you. overlooking.
my voice, caught. the shape of an unknown thing.

what is it? this self. this space. between the seer and the seen.
like a river. *or a window.* opening. *animal.* dark.

you are floating in circles. eyes closed. arms wide. unbound then.
from inside the shadows of the trees. she slips. out. *malvaceae, solanaceae, violaceae.*

—as if to name herself. by the shore of the stream. *apparition. wild.*
turning. turns. looks at me.

then at you. —*the archeress of forests and hills.*

       my dear, some things are certain.
it is noon.

I am blinded by the gleaming of the leaves.
fabaceae, liliaceae, orchidaceae.

I haven't moved, I haven't breathed, when you, splashing,
set your feet, stand, waterdrops flashing off your shoulders and arms and hair—

look straight into my eyes.
tell it if you can.

I

And within the deepest shade,
the innermost recess, there lay a cave
most perfect.

—Ovid, *The Metamorphoses, Actaeon*

in the beginning

you sit in the light on the greenhouse floor
stretched over your notes and the warm brick

and the angles flashing across the brightness and
the pine wood tables and the willow-cut baskets of earth.

a pale green haze rises out of the seed flats.
at first, he lingers at the window, as if to decide, —

    suddenly flocked. the colors. the raw shape of it
between us awkward leaping: caught.

                then—*once upon a time. long, long ago...*

the history of a color

you can see it where the pathway bends into the hills, across the contour, rising.
all the grass in seed and thick between the ruts and where the road falls off.

cowfields. a wooden gate.
hedgerows mark the water lines.

everyone is calling. the skies darken. piling into the north.

*

no single color in the chromatic range of green
        appears in Neolithic painting.

and the glaucous sea
        is the same shade to Odysseus

as Calypso's glaucous eyes, as the glaucous underside of the leaves in her orchard,
        as the shimmering honey she makes

—a sweet paleness there.

*

lying on our backs in the dirt by the summer-ditch
        we can hear it.

there is nothing in between. the air and the body itself
    gray-barked, riven and wet and filled with its voices.

a shelter, close as skin.

*

Goethe says darkness is not the absence
        of light, but rather

        another kind of wave, like light,

complementary, as mind is to heart.

   —color comes from holding hands,
  the warmth that rises in between.

*

a pair of salamanders
   suspended in the lake
  in the middle place

woven into the seam binding night and day—

columns of gold
   descend into the water,
  deep into the heart.

still. as a match.

*

then viridis appears, and a whole family of names to mean the luminosity resident in things:
viridine, viridescence, verdance, verdure, verdet rising from within. the way knowing feels

before speaking can begin.

*

at first, I couldn't see.
  I couldn't tell between the mirror and the gaze, your fleeting eyes.
  the glance. your sunlit arms.

it doesn't matter.
  you were here. a sudden fluency—

eyes closed windows flung wide
  and the wind so near and ready and the brilliant canopies of leaves

 and the sudden rain pouring straight down in.

ink

we began to write, he said.
to each other, she said. each day. in journals that we shared.

so that we wrote in response to the letter we had just received on the letter itself, he said.
we had two, she said. two at once. correspondences.

what I loved best, he said, is the way you wrote over my words.
so that our sentences tangled.

sometimes, she said, we filled pages with ink.
till it was like a net. or looking up into the trees.

and each morning when we exchanged what we had written,—
I could feel you there, inside the body of your words, he said, reaching out,

like a pathway, lit from within, opening. to a clearing you had made. for me.
it was like falling in.

it is said that reading requires the reader to acquire a self.
and that this selfness is an edge.

so that something lies between the world and our imagination of it.
the way all language is a veil.

but this was different.

what we made was a place we could hold,
he said. a place we could be. inside.

like the sill of a window, open
she said. in a room that we painted together, he said.

side-by-side, in a garden, on a hill
watching for the birds.

and for the weather that we made, she said.

to hatch

at first, it's something broken makes me look, the sharp, small flake like a tear in the grass.
and then it's the color.

we look up. *nestlings!*

*

Sunday. near the beginning, I left my car in a ditch, tore my shirt on the fence
then slept in the grass, hidden till the moon rose and the sky turned violet

and the voices trailing out of the wind, pinned me to the ground. tell me a story, they said.

*

Monday. once there was a girl named Sophia. she was normal in every way but for the arrow in her eye.
over time the arrow grew and the world darkened. of course, she could not see it because it was hers
and because it slept in her eye. one day, in the way that revelation always happens, she caught a glimpse
of herself sidelong in the milliner's shop-window and she saw: the arrow like a wing with its mallard fletches
nesting beautifully there, in her eye. at first she felt shock, then shame, then a fear close to terror. and now,
what is she to do? the world is a wonder, unfixed and unknown. the self in it too. what if she recognizes
nothing? what if bloodied and blinking she wakes herself blind? having named the thing beside her
that darkens, can it be removed?

*

once, I found myself walking down the street. black asphalt. like tarmac.
on the right, a city park with elms, evenly spaced. on the left, a sidewalk,
bright windows, dry goods, women's shoes. in the middle of the road,
there's a manhole missing its cover. I leap in and fall.
at the bottom, I find myself sitting in a rich black earth.
I see with my hands. I touch the roots. I smell the good dirt.
later, I climb out and find myself walking down the street.
black asphalt. like tarmac. on the right, a city park, green with elms
and lawn. on the left, a sidewalk, windows, candles made of beeswax.
in the middle of the road, there's a hole. it is very dark and I cannot see,
but for the love of leaping, I leap in.

at the bottom, I find myself sitting in a rich black earth.
I see with my hands. it is moist and warm and I want it to fit.
I want to taste. later, I find myself walking down a street.
it is night. the city lights are like stars. there is a hole pulling me in.
I leap.

*

circling. circling. dawnlight. a bear on the path in my dreams.

*

late now. Tuesday. too soon. the mayflies
rise at dusk from out of the rocks, into the current, peeling themselves

through the veils at the water's surfaces.

*

Wednesday. something happens at the end of winter, a swirling time, when spring threatens to wake us all, and the wind blows its ruse and its danger: 'come out if you dare.' the darkness is leaving.

I'm afraid I've lost everything.

*

once, I went looking for the elk beneath the ridge in the flats by the creek:
a young bull asleep in the grass. when he woke to my walking, he stood.

and for a minute he stared, not moving.

*

*Thursday. once in a winter desert. hard rain deep.
I am flooded and flooding. unraveled. unleashed.*

pine dropseed. mountain muhly. junegrass. sweetgrass. wild manna grass—
suddenly, he bursts into flight.

again and again. a madness of water.
of heat.

*

Friday morning. the garden window's open, binding us to it.
—eggshell blue, like that.

Saturday. nested.
little wing. clouded.

rising. to a hard rain deep.

it was a gift. the night. the sky. the wind.
it was a story. *a kiss.* like permission. *unfolding.*

there are fishes in the story. side-by-side. a crimson thread.

we watched from the bridge. into the currents. a green bus. and a girl. cold
above the tree line. —we were hunting for ptarmigan

in the season that fades from mottled-brown to white and the snow deepens.
in pools against the rocks.

*

there's a torrent at the crossing. unexpected. mineral-carved canyonslide
we pull over. searching. for the voices. for the birth. for the fall.

*

once, my father gathered me into his arms before dawn and we drove to the river.
I wake to the mist curling back across the waters and the sun flashing
and I am blind-casting into the wildlight and leaning toward that sudden pull my heart
racing.

*

voice, tongue, lips in the wet world under—
fluid and scaled and cold. is that speaking?

to be finned and gilled and tailed and giddy and longing. to be painted?
in a body? IS that?

*

some far slip. some whispered rut. cut across the contour. and the summer dirt. powder.
electric. or— touch. and it pearls away, a voice no more than air.

if you lie in the sand and stare straight, you can feel
how the water shapes it. how it braids. sifting. something not broke.

something that cannot break. how everything fits. everything's wave.

*

once, I was a mermaid in the pool in the summer
surrounded by a million screaming somebodies, and yet
beautifully alone. infinite. chlorinated. blue.

*

we stand in the eddy. at the fault line.
a bay-colored rock. laid in sheaves so that it breaks horizontal.

first snow—first flakes. twisting. one-by-one.

what falls away is a gesture into. scree into pine into prairie.
green into blue into white.

you can feel it. the winter's night. coming in. coming through.

*

some nights I dive down there to speak
some nights I tell myself stories to make myself weep—
then, let the tides stroke my hair. [I stroke my own hair, till I fall
myself to sleep].

*

some nights the lake is gray, or burnished like steel or mist or flat. opaque. repeating.
black. with the barest light on top. warmer than air. I am swimming in between.
liquid. not.

some nights I am woven. and in it.

*

my voice is in the crests. waiting for the when in which I want them,
see them, love them—
wish to speak, and you will speak, girl.
wish to die, and you can do it—foam only.
wish to live, and here you are—aquatic and electric and abuzz—

*

in the story there's a crossing. sunhot. rock-gleam. the animal river.
wish to speak and my feet are rooted.

—all the pathways meeting here.

*

[in the days when wishing is having, I get what I wish for, and then I wish I hadn't]
I want the jungle-lushness rainstorm in my heart, marsh birds
on my tongue I want
to be so quicksilvered so flash-flooded up-filled
that I overflow
that I mudflow spill it
without
fear of parching, fear of perishing for the lack,
for the lack alack alack—

and what is it that you long for that you cannot have?

*

tracks at the soft edge. heron here. pressed it. creased this. waited, stepped here
waded, watchful. the water pulls me deeper in. the little silt waves asking

if I want to be taken.

*

the cold of it.
waking
the inside-out of it. oiling in fin and bone—
the slick of it. the smooth-sticky swim of it
eeling
upcurrent, in wave, upstream, in slither—in deep

*

and the bird, this heron, quickly sharp now

lifts—till her wings, outstretched, for the slightest moment—slips

to the heat of it—leaps, to the radiance—the sweet bright curve of it—
bent now, curls now—lifting, up—

*

to the backlit wingspray streaming
streamfew, droplight [having flown once...]
dripfall, wet, falling, [having fallen]—from out of no place, from out of nothing—
to the mind dark, rock dark, wet now—

*

to the heat of it. parsing and pouring and leaving—and dazzling.
to the want of it. —I want to come in.

the blue beetle

once, making a fence with our arms in the grass
your body long against my side—

how like a wave the end of July breaks. and you.
my tempest of light.

la grâce d'un vol

tell me where to begin—
by the waters—

sunlight falls through the leaves, brightens the gravel.
there's moss on the rocks by the creek. a deep pool.

you are my lost-found wild-child. eternally hatching.
and you, my mirror.

I'm trying to see what kind of 'winged' I am.
dragonfly. damselfly. flying-fish.

yes, it's the form I question, the costume.
whether it's given, or made?

—or shockingly accidental!
as chestnut stamens now strewn everywhere across

the rocks. streamers in the water. a pendulous confetti
—sorrows pealing from the sky.

and beautiful because. the simple rain. given to the wind. *—but no!*
shouldn't we say 'leaf-wings' 'soaring' then? to land? —because we want the falling to be flight?

'comme elles tombent bien!' everything's drawn in. *a secret love!*
as water bends around the rocks, again

—it makes a kind of bridge. step-by-step.

my feet in sunlight now, —how I would stay.
to watch the hatch? the fading too?

to see what we become.
a wildness unbound—

a chorus of waters
spirals and falls and eddies and leaves

—and this tiny fish, this speckled dace that I can see, only now?

—*she is so much within*—the fabric of the stream—until—
the veil, lifted, —did she 'decide' for me to see?

she is herself. most truly. and holds to her lines and sways at the edge
as if to catch some thinner thread. then flashes sometimes quick

toward nothing I can see. and back again. *glittering text! she's stitching something in.*
and if she disappears because I move too quick?

because you want to swim? alone together? —in the story of water, my dear, a thrill hums in everything
—you, me—the mayfly's sticky wings—

the art of collage

choose your color. fold the page. fold again.
now. tear from the corners.

if you lie level with the water at dusk, at the very edge, you can see the hatch.
tiny white sails peel through the surfaces, then float, clear for a moment,—

then leap into the air.

make crescents and circles and squares.
make triangles. save the pieces.

sometimes you come to a place where the pinecones have fallen together
into a shallow bowl. fitted perfectly to the curve of the ground. as if they had been calling

each-to-each. one-and-one-and-one.

make a pile of the shapes and colors. let them drift. let them settle.
the days may pass. then weeks.

you might decide to stay. by the creekbank. to name the shallows, the greens.
sometimes you find a strangeness there. sometimes it comes in torrents.

and when you return. after the rain. look for the shapes that fit. the colors that glow. side-by-side.
look at the edges.

once, I caught a fish, far and high away. the country was granite
and pine. the waters made amber by the gravel inside.

look where the fibers come loose. sometimes clustered together. sometimes crosswise, overlapping.
the tear is ragged, uneven. look how the texture of the page rises from within.

brook trout. gravid. barely the length of my hand. a flashing white streak
at the edge of the fin. and then a thin black line. and then crimson.

there's a landscape inside. contour. look: you can see where the cut softens
at the edge. where the paper comes undone. it beckons. into the space between

as if to reach across. leaning. toward and through.

and something else. —something muscular and strong. fluid
and wild. —her body pours into the hollows.

take these. and the stream-colored light. —the pathway's circling.
—and falling the way it does through the trees.

beginning, fragments

I've seen the deer by the creekbank rise
like wind and flame upward together.

pine leaves fallen into sweetgrass
by the edge of the barn.

I didn't tell you for a long time.
but I knew the sound. broken. unbroken.

it's like a map, you said.
the crescent moon. the geese at twilight.

the shadows of the branches of the trees.
written. and close.

the lake, only water

you wait for me at the shore, curled up in the grass,
thin as a moon wrapped in your towel.

we paddle together to the dock and sit in the sun.
the swallows come out. you slip into the lake and swim.

angular arms, sunlight flashing, easy, elemental.
and then you change direction at right angles to yourself, crossing

and re-crossing your own wake and I wonder if you are writing to the birds,
what you are trying to say. I love how the lake holds you.

and there I am, in the late afternoon, in the middle of nowhere, in the middle of my life
watching you speak in some ritual language, the language of women, of birds, the language

of water, as you pull yourself, glittering, up and out—laughing—
and I cannot look away.

deciduous

in every story there's a moment
the silence of water on skin

a shadow-ripple just beneath the eddy's spiral
sunlight at the surfaces

so that the leaf becomes a text, a constellation
the silence between words

a fearful beauty
the silence of the rain

the memory of flight
a window

not particular to a landscape of rock or tree or water
a birth, a claim, only

a self, a body
the silence of your glance

something winged
looking into, and across

the landscape of waiting
the colors refracted

the leaving
sewn in

subtext

a window in the greenroom. a garden of trees.
   the opal sky. fractals of gold and violet.

two salamanders suspended above the formless dark.
   liquid. speaking.

November. late afternoon. the light
   wraps itself into everything it touches.

the riverbark, the templed lake.
   a language of eyes and shoulders and cadence and pitch.

as the leaves fall there's a music underneath
   of bells. then a flock of tiny birds. or,

not a flock, maybe three, maybe two small voices. moving. tree to tree.
   looking up, how like seamstresses they seem. making this, making that.

songlines. elemental. as if to wake each leaf.
   the story has a smooth-ish, sensical skin, a lettering.

a body, reflected.
   a note held. then still. as a picture of things.

or a window in. branch to branch. knotting air to shadow.
   making room. *a kind of sound-beingness.*

—but can it stay? can a word ever BE itself? simple, pure?
   —or, so filled with naming, can we only ever hear the barest traces of ourselves?

it's snowing again. this fragile agreement. the trees whiten. I wake to despair
   turning inside-out as if to follow the light till nothing is there—

this place that was so filled with green.

once I was a bird.

in the sweetapple tree.

singing and singing just for the sky.

then winter comes. the apples fall.

and the wind on the water calls and calls.

the tempest

my head is full of noises—
tell me! this question you ask—would you be haunted? hunted?

I know the black, the white, the shades of gray—
but this spindle, masked—

storm, without instruction or pretense to pray
I do not know what to do—

then let them gust away your bones
rather ravaged by unforgiveness, some foreign

ferocious color—than be untouched—

but—I cannot even hear the wind—

    and this to me—
the brilliance and beauty of the sun—desire has allotted

—for all the swirling, beating light

the sweetapple tree

honey—being—being
I was a stronger version of myself
in that nectar place—winged-girl in the wild flowers—

I wake in someone else's body. we buy chocolate, take a tram.
looking out the windows. the traffic keeps me locked inside.

crevices of cabinets for my slow spoonfuls—sipped—
makes me light, sweeter than—

sometimes, I want to say to you—

lemon. ginger. cayenne.

how far we've wandered. the streets compressed with heat and strange.
how much together—this garden of trees—how close, we—

Stop.

you know this already. the story we made. high on the highest branch.
and its leaves and the rain

and the maps. what cannot be undone. and you, now —forgot? or,
—unable to reach?   please.

you must tell it if you can.

how slowly the canvas awnings, the poles, the broken racks and cord, the tables
stacked, the dreary space, the street's leavings come undone.

how slowly concrete decays in the heat. first, the colored paint
then grain-by-grain corrodes.

severance

april: to hatch

in the beginning, you cross the bridge, alone, toward your first love.
the river is hardly speaking, but it feels the long pull.
you hold hands, kiss in the woods, and summer-comes.
everything in the world is held between.

the windows open wide.
the hardwood floors in a room full of light, faraway, in a house on the hill.

may: subtext

once, inside the voices and the glitter at the celebration luncheon, as you talked, I watched
your left-hand palm-up resting over the green silk dress in folds across your lap
like a boat on the sea. your right hand lay on the table mapping the single-creviced edge
of the silver butter knife. almost a caress. rhythmic. you were a compass pointing north,
northeast.

june: water

I dreamed we were salamanders and you said, *I will teach you to float.*
and so, one day, in the middle of the lake, we let the boat drift away.
without touching, you said, *tip your head back. throw your arms out wide; let your hips rise.*
it feels like a swan dive back, and—all I can see is blue. suspended in the sky.
held up to the very edge of this liquid earth. your voice across the water inside me. laughing.
level with the waves. my heart. loved like that.

july: water

the light on your skin breaks into amber, violet, lavender, green. fractures at the curve
of your hip and the shadows drawing in. something electric there between you

and the simple air. we are drying in the sun, talking, and I say what I see.
that you are made of light. that I am falling in. a line I can never cross.
should never have crossed.

august: deciduous

it came as a map. a survey of lines. a letter. that you read aloud. a distance written in. a stop.
in this country, drought makes things resinous. longing is dust hardened with sap.
piñon. juniper. sage. you touched my hand. *it is a map*, you said. my thirst growing like wind.

it feels a kind of fire. a lie. sedimentary. mine.

september: ink

I hadn't noticed before. our letters held their silences.
and though we both entered, alone, together, it was not a place we could actually go.
it was a room in our hearts we had made. with separate doors. I watched the yellow warblers
come and leave. I made you presents I could not give, and then the ravens.

I think of you in the morning light writing your last note, the tea and the honey,
the pressed flowers, your reticence. but you spoke what I could not. *there is no going back.*
and then it was just me.

december: tempest

once, you held your hand to my back, and I could feel the sun, and I knew
that you could never leave. and once, shoulder to shoulder, I could feel the gravity
between us, and that we were bound together in a way I could not speak.

but I was a swarm of locusts in a blizzard with nowhere to land.
one by one, I fell out of the sky.

may: severance

you asked what I wanted. as if I could say. as if naming could make it possible.
but I cannot.

and you, wiser than me, nod, then smile, then turn, then walk into the light of the day.

january: paris

otherwise, the sky
would be white as the inside rooms of spring

a wind across the steppe
a silvered roof, bare arms, outstretched.

instead, the rowan tree with her crimson scarves
turns on her heel, whirls away. again.

II

Artemis half-revealed caught up her dress and encircling shawl, and sank with gliding limbs into the water, until by little and little all her form was hidden.

—Nonnos, *Dionysiaca*

The branches that he parted to get a better view
now grew in the place of eyes.

—Norman O. Brown, *Apocalypse and/or Metamorphosis*

Do we get another life?   *Oh yes.*
Maybe not in this place.   *Maybe in different forms.*

—Jean Valentine, *Diana*

the mirrors of Actaeon:

(summer's end)

each morning the swifts return from underground
to feed their raucousness, to calibrate the sky

and more and more it's noon all day. there was barking, yes.
a distant rumble as in falling rock, and then the pause.

*

look how the skin folds
downward splotchy burnt
like grease fire in the rue fields

escarpment scraped and breathless still

who could be in there? furtive and scuffling—
what in God's name could be in there?
pining behind the sofa like that

*

days and weeks I can't find you. though it rains.
we died in a moonlit sky.

the rocks cut through my ribs—our bones like little boats balanced on the ground
and the wind inside—we were told to wait

for spring, or something to melt, a color. a kind of rose.
and then a dog appeared, stole my arm in his teeth.

I could not move. I could not speak
till the seashells in my throat shook me awake, and the dog leapt with my humerus, racing

downhill. you were your usual wraithful self. annoyed at my persistence, my endless decay.
ghostlike, twisting, you turned yourself to wend your way from out of me.

I was cavernous then, face up into the rain.
—how lovely the blue of it felt on my head, my eyes open endlessly, my mouth

a ruin. having eaten all there is.

*

for wreckage like me there's no hope but the crows, dispersal
and a metric kind of thinking—they know all my sinews by name.

we come apart in pieces, delicate, their bills along the thread lines, follow
the grain, then fold me up with colored stones and cache me under the cactus spines.

ravens only rip. coyotes live to tear, obsequious and slovenly.
the mice and the maggots—that low inharmonious hum.

*

a wave at the edge of the sky. rootlike, sculptural. blue on blue. thin as bone.

(a winter constellation)

Orion rises, snores beside me
filling the dog dish
like the sea its wild abundance
and I'm nothing but flotsam and skin
a minor volition. oh, sing to me dear.

—quick! we are all of it drowning!

*

waiting for the blizzard I
notice that my left shoulder's tallest
and my mouth is bent I
think maybe he doesn't breathe
properly on account of that tractor
crashing in his youth or maybe he's
just a gelding took a two-by-four but I
can't quite figure why that pinch
in the corner of his face begs for rain like
something might've died or he's got
a trick-tank broke all algae and slick
and broiling amongst the crevices I think
he thinks he's fancy thinks he's
quick waits to say: no. —darling
it's only sugar in the pines.

*

you look fine.
that's what he says but I know
what he thinks pointing at his empty self oh, closet!
—nothing but grackles and sticks.

*

today, I'm a landscape with hills and a stab of light right through the middle

into the fat part where the trees are. I'm cut in two and all the leaves are coming out.
it might rain. it could be muddy. it might could always snow again.

*

stop
we're neither of us spring chickens
anymore like all the succulence went packing
for a trip to mango-land is what I think
later in the day after catching him sneak a peek at
that newfound double-chin, like what's that you're holding in your craw, dude
like you're afraid of getting hit and all the world's a trick
but I woke early and killed a mouse panicked
crossing the road in the snow even though I bought
new tires to keep from sledding but nothing against
that tiny white skittering oh shit
and now it's nothing but a pint of slush and blood
waiting for the morning and the ravens
and I do not think I can.

*

I want to tell the truth.
the sky is blue like a drain
full of crows. green's just a wish.
the wind hasn't come. we're huddled round
the fishing hole, me and myself, keeping warm at the stove.
I'm waiting, I guess. such nice electric coils so perfectly coiled
I could brand myself by taking a nap. maybe
Van Gogh would come out. maybe I could make
Starry Nights with my face. I could lose an ear. yes,
I'm listening too. for you. it's not that. —don't you see? all of this blue
swimming round and round
—and nothing left to do?

(paris, saint valentine's day)

the houses lean back, narrow, bound together.
ravens at the drainpipes. cobblestone. archways. shutters flung wide.
starlings by the hedges. a pair of mallards in the ivy in the sunlight on a wall.
seagulls under the bridges. a winter's scaffolding.

everything's uneven. unframed. paint bleeds across the canvas, across the beams.
at the island's downstream edge, the river eddies in on itself
saying and saying, all afternoon, *it is late afternoon.* as if lit from within
holding nothing. and the light is plain. bright and gray. curling in. folding in.

this great glittering city.

a fisherman lifts a silver fish from the hold of his boat for his boy to see. ropes coiled against
the planking inside. and the waves break along the wooden hull, run and run to the pier.

(mistral)

wood smoke breaks horizontal from the priest's house chimney.
a smudge at the waist of the scene.

the elms, not from here either—still
impossibly wild.

*

everything's peeled and broken. the gutter's skin-hoard clatters west.
a caravan of wind. nothing fits.

*

Thursday—
and Clarity has not yet arrived.

wind and dust and snow and dust.

and wind.

(in the hall of dogs)

I want names.

as if to raise the dead.
as if to speak in tongues.
the pathway in, rooted, bent, dumb...

Amarynthus, Arcena, Borax, Aethon
Corus, Dromas, Labros, Lacon

Melampus, Omargus, Syrus, Theron
Thoos, Tigris, Hylactor, Ladon

my. such big teeth we have. gnarled and falling. caked.
the better to eat. you with. my dear.

nothing moves. even their eyes.

even the magpies are gone.

(by the waters)

the sedges billow over the banks
then lay themselves flat into the current.

a gesture of giving. *carex aquatilis.* or *pellita. utriculata.*
like heron tracks. see what we've made? with our long wide blades?

there's a bear in the woods. by the bridge. sending us side-long glances.
we're fixing cabinets. three wooden steps. a porch needing paint.

the screen door's open. she's fat as a yawn. ambles into the house.
he thinks to photograph the stain-glass transom, as if to mark the way:

window with bear. —when she disappears. inside it. just like that—we're left
standing under the architecture staring at the place

where the current disappears.

(april's casement)

I don't believe a
thing my body says to me
like eat chocolate
love you because he's just a
window filled with trinkets shiny
knobs hinges painted butter-
flies and a blue you can't get
here from there. I promise—
break the glass and all your beauties
fly away

*

I'm working on not-waiting
it's like waiting but without the pictures
so you run into things and then forget
she said I lean too much on lack—
I don't even know what shoe to drop or where we are in the hymn
like an endless snake-in-a-snake
or a bowlful of cherries
they're all gone someplace else—
and now it's starting to snow again and I'm
still swimming uphill not-waiting at all
in the still not-yet quite-dark

*

the light is brightest at his head
like rosebuds at noon
I can see the aphids from here
surrounded by ants
but the shrubbery is dark as knees, the middle places
barely lit. still, the dogs are at his feet
dreaming mint pistachio ice cream dreams
always cold and sweet

(mirror, mirror)

the space inside constraint's
sweet closet—expands, again—
 windows in the roses
blue-stained and winged. still.
a continent lies between.

*

I'm in a room full of nudes
in a workplace environment
but only their backsides are shown—
they are half-men turning like Chirons at the copier
marble statues of professors professing
just as the light reflected off the primmest hedge
in Dallas in March seems green and gold
and pink at once window glass
protecting what it sees—
visible invisible I
take off my clothes and step into the aftermath.

*

on a roadway in a roadster in the hills bearing south to the coast
through an opening in the trees past the grass, past the rise to a broken rest-stop
in an oak-wooded ravine to get a coke. as if I know this place.

looking back, looking up across the distance into the light
there's a hawk cuts a line straight through.

*

I decided to go with the girls because I could not bear the gaps.
we rode shotgun to town in a shopping cart (pointed like a ruby slipper)
raised above the tarmac on a levered arm, the laughter of texts
and the forces of yellow, palatable and good—

in another panel, the intersection of witches takes place in a sunburnt sky
under black and round-brimmed hats.
flames darken the west.

(once)

a patch of light
along the bark of the plane tree
 sighs like an anemone in a tide pool.
and now, suddenly—everyone's free.

*

remember:
tear from the corners.

sleet on the roof.
the lake in the wind.
the color of sycamore leaves.

the causes of decay

curled up and by me, entwined. your legs drawn in
laughing, like a bird

and the veil drawn over, between.

I want to be alone. or,

with you. like eggshells, or

deceit. that outward face

in. I remember so clearly two worlds. I was split in half, and no one knew, or,

late now. snow moon. waiting and waiting.

*

gas cap
toothpaste
drive to the plains
walk
sleep
read
write
walk

*

finally home. a tangle of women swim toward me swirling, the mysterious one leaving,
returning, she is young and pretty, and I want her; she asks to marry on the weekend,
and I say yes, excited because she is dressed in flowers and all will be well.
but then I remember I am already married, and on the way to the church I am late,
and I have to work, and I have to tell her, and I think about calling, but I think I should
tell her in person, and I am still trying to catch a yellowcab, or should I walk?
or take a tram? or marry both? and what would she say, and what would *She* say, and the sky

is blue and dressed in white lace in the San Gabriel mission in an old Spanish town, like LA, because she is Catholic and we must marry in the church of our mothers.

*

the door to the house is ripped from its skin. light
streams into the foyer across the tiles, reflected off the mirror,
through the cracks on either side. unhinged. the wood is splintered. torn.

I can't put it back. it won't close. won't lock.
tipped to the jam. it won't fix.

and the light pours out in sheets.

*

I wake up thinking about sex with strangers. it's alienating.
the sky is blue. the garden's thirsty. hot.
centered like that. pelvis to pelvis how perfectly we fit.
lips in my mouth. the better to speak you with my dear. feel something.
heat rising. I want to be inside.

pink salt dust clings to the crystal salt boat.
a kind of desert on the glass. a perfect storm.

*

apples
avocados
cheese
pasta
scallions
blueberries
wine
Baudelaire

*

you hold the pencils like a knife twisting, drawing down toward your body

laying paint in long sinuous lines. these are trees, a garden of trees.
each slowly thickening. as if to carve the space between, as if the colors
in their lanes slowly urging something from within sculpting ribbons, sunlight,
wind. shiraz, bronze, sienna, then scarlet lake and crimson lake and deep vermillion.
the edges of allure. what happens when you cross.

*

we walk together side by side, in a dark set of rooms
a hallway, in an evening place. not a city
but chandeliered, with noises in the walls. a catacomb. cut-rock and shadowed.
to a gathering of names. pinned and yellow with voices.
we are standing at the wall, choosing.

and then you are leaving again. your long legs striding into the cobbled dark.

*

a psalm of sedges:

obtuse	loving	clustered	needleleaf
dryspike	western	mountain	little wing
sun	analogue	woolly	water

*

because of the war
we hide in the bed inside
a wooden frame, buried
under blankets—
stay low—
you press against me curl
your hands into my back
so that
your narrow hips lock
into mine and your skin
waits.
still.

*

I trace the length of your spine to the sacrum and think how oddly shaped you seem. how frail and human, that the skin and bones beneath are bent, singular, heading toward overuse, a kind of wear in the form, a triangular stone for making wishes. there, pressed into you, toward the idea of you, how possibility still waits, even with this lurking dis-integration, there is still light, as if from inside. you smile. dark blue skies bearing rain and the long blonde streamers in waves off the dropseed, like whitecaps on a sandy sea.

*

I tell all my stories to the flame at the small of your back
in a circular script

side by side.
we are wrapped in leaves—lemon, butter, salt.

III

Still to this day, some evenings I hear a voice calling me by name in the street. A somewhat husky voice. It drags a bit around certain syllables, and I recognize it immediately. I turn around but there's nobody there. Not only in the evenings but during that sluggish part of those summer afternoons when you're no longer even sure what year it is.

I often hear that voice in my dreams.

—Patrick Modiano, *In the Café of Lost Youth*

She came without sound,
Without brushing the stones,
In the soft dark of early evening,
She came,
The wind in her hair,
The moon beginning.

—Theodore Roethke, *The Visitant*

postcard, artemisia

in the story you were leaving again. but we were side by side, getting ready.
you were dressed in blue. and we are shoulder to shoulder then, quiet working.

I've traced you a card and filled it with color, but only the greens. the emeralds and moss
and the ferns. that place it shifts into wave and we're both falling in.

but here—the hills lean toward yellow, or shale and rust, as if all day were afternoon
in a south-facing ravine. still. the swallows are long-winged and strange.

it's a kind of prayer: myrtle, teal, jade. like celadon, cerulean. or turquoise, malachite.
then laurel, alder, chestnut, pine. willow, rush. sweetgrass. sage.

postcard, subtext

dear traveler. dearest friend, remember the pictures we found of the swimmers in the sea?
looking up from below, from underneath, the watery greens—and their bodies—even then!
holding nothing. so lithe and alive. look how they move, how like the currents
they've become. never–still.

then gliding together again into the waves.
then suddenly wave.

then suddenly foam again together
into the bright air.

tell the story

I don't understand.
once upon a time...

...by the long rows. lines of dark, blue-black machines. like trains. between us. blocking.
we're in a station. with its glass and its clouds. I'm leaving. you hurry away

through the clamor and the steam. I'm standing alone at the quay
with my bags.

I don't know which train to take.

—*yes.*
I long for something green. the countryside. the fields. —you seem like the wind.

I need to put my hands in the dirt. I need my feet in the earth.
I need to make it rain.

to hatch, new moon

she is everywhere around me. in the kitchen. on the porch.
walking by the lake. in the light on the stage. at the spring.

it's not obsession. more like a wood-shaving from a hand-plane:
the cut, sharp, stings, then rides into
the smell of pine, curling in and in, till it's tight. pinned.

*

sometimes I look through the window
listen for the quiet inside her house
listen for the slightest breath, but nothing moves
not even the light on the dust, not even the dust.

*

they lie side by side on the bridge.
from here, all you can see is their legs dangling
over the edge, bare feet dragging in the stream.
she points at the sky. he's feeling the heat
of her waist too close.

elsewhere, the girls are in the woods. laughter rises out of the willows. marsh wrens
in orbit.

*

she's holding my sweater and pointing to the hole, the unraveling.
it's my father's, Irish navy blue. as she holds it up, her hand falls through

an opening in the shoulder, and I can see the un-doings. it's coming apart at the seams.
she says, *100% wool; you should fix it.*

I don't know how. but then, I imagine a red stitching at the edges
and the colors vibrate together, and the fibers glisten,

and she draws me close to press her body to mine, to lean her whole self against me,
and I am trying to feel what she means—

as if I could read her pressing like the words in a book, but I am holding my breath.
she whispers *stay*, and suddenly my face in her hair I am ravenous to be inside.

I wonder what the sweater means, how I will sew these threads with my bare hands.

*

she's in the house, clear-eyed and kissing. I fall asleep in the chair and wake
to find her in the bed. but everyone's stirring. time to leave. looking out through the door
to the hall, the family gets ready for school. we watch.

—and the boy and his mother knock to come in.

I divert them away to the kitchen so you can leave. your silhouette in the dark behind me,—
your body's the moon. pulling me out. holding me in.

the least wave

we're travelling together downstream.
barefoot. along the river. along the dry, cobbled edge. late summer.
I am trying to recall to you the first beach: a steep slope of sand.
the sudden deep water. the slip of it.

you turn to look at me. press your forehead to mine. then slow
you trace the bones of my face with your cheek. with your chin. till we are leaning
against each other. till we fall into a strange orbit. your head perfectly fitted
to the circle of my shoulder. we are slow wooden gears. each
twist seeking into the hollows of the other. I am
helping you to turn. my hand
slips to your waist. to the curve of your hip.

I can feel you then. the bones inside. listening.
how you rise to meet. the expanse of you
unfolding. —I have no ground.
I cannot tell if you know.
or why you move against me. into me. the way you do.

the beach in my story is far from here.
a circling I can't seem to unwind.
and yet all the surfaces are shining:

the river spinning past.
the sweetnesses of the sand.
the willows. my tempest.

please. begin
again.

calypso

once upon a time across the sands— it's like a window.
a long boat, leaving. the way it pulls. this 'once.'

yes. supple and wide. muscular and still.
—she's sleeping. the dawn-light's coming.

it's near and warm. yet something's underneath...
she's breathing slow. look how full she lies. *and yet—*

the wind! —yes, calling her to move, begging
'wake please!' —*and look how she abides*

from crest to slip to swell, again, again. I think she loves the light,
the air's insistent hands—the wind is everywhere she goes.

the voice inside her.
          —*and so, my dear, what of this 'long boat, leaving?'*

we're facing west, and into. the waves are high.
but see how much there is?

it feels an edge. —yes. and we gaze down, upon, from high beyond.
it's a leap, a flight! —but look how we cannot,

how—we are rooted in this frame, leaning out, but bound—
No! —*look at how she sees: that sweet, sweet glance, the dark*

lingering, that heat, 'how much there is!'
look—she's lifting, turning, her voice clear—and we—look!

now slipping, about to slip—

the bear, and other adventures

she arrives at the house with three small cubs, so small
they could fit into the palm of your hand.

she noses around the siding.
we watch from the living room window. a watery glass.

till she finds a crack
then comes looking, room to room. for me.

her great arched back, her golden shoulder, fill the hall. patient.
curious. she ambles past the bedroom door.

I sneak out, and down, and toward the stairs, my hand on the banister,
imagining the kitchen, the screen-door slam,

and then she turns, and I am pinned against the wall.

—there is a moment, touching her ribs, her back, her thighs. this rich land,
when I know with perfect clarity, I will not survive.

*

six dead snakes hang by their heads from hooks on a wall, a rack.
dark black, I can't see the pattern, but they're rattlesnakes.

we're measuring but have no ruler. I make one. from paper. in millimeters.
it goes to six. I have to measure by marking the spot on each snake each time.

six, plus six, plus six, like this.

they are dead. here is where my finger comes close but does not touch.
a glistening of scales. of gold and red and pink. not much. just a hint. I do not touch.

*

there's a bird in the parking lot with a broken wing flapping in circles on its back, yellow

olive-green. you text me pictures of yourself from behind, little message screens, first
your shoulder, then the back of your head with your hair peeking out.
a café table and a glass of wine.

then in braids you turn away, flashing with maroon in it.
I want. to be. with you.

but I can't seem to get out of the parking lot. with the miserable dying bird.
I can't seem to get this picture of you, straight.

*

the bear sits in the front seat of our rental car. strapped in. looks
straight-ahead. I wonder what to do.

I could sell windows.

it's not like this has never happened in the history of love.
the frame changes everything.
the veil is like a glass.
you might be emerald-green today.
I might invent the wheel.
but what of you? can I ever know?

and now, again—

—you said *we must be fierce. grief is indulgence.*
thresholds have been crossed. careful what you eat.

maybe, I should just shut up and drive.

the veils (*viola adunca*)

I find a wasp in the morning in the sink and put her on the sill. she preens. each of her six legs, one-by-one, then nods as I lean in. the gesture I know exactly as acknowledgment.

but what do I know?

her abdomen is built of scales, rounded plates that slide
one into the next like shells. a carousel of yellow gifts.

she taps her sting. each limb jointed. seven times.
a spikelet at her wrist to catch the drops. to peel the droplets from her legs.

I take her on my finger. feel her press against my skin.
there is no other language.

rain on the glass.
magpies in the trees in the morning.

*

the book of violets opens.
it is dusk.

pressed in newsprint, there are two.
two flowering stems. made to overlap

so that they form an interlocking
s. the flowers lean away, but their bodies

lie together in a bed of leaves.

*

she hovers from window to sill. across the room, through intersecting panes of light.
for a moment she holds completely still. a point in air. her wings ablur. amber. ochre.

her legs hang loose, hieroglyphic. and then she slips from light to dark.
a shimmer. then nothing's there. the wave and the raft.

a rising to meet. a falling away. tiny hooks for toes.

*

in the story, the bull is led to the temple. in procession.
he is draped in violets. the people watch.

he looks out as if through a window.

they wait. and they watch. to see whether the world will brighten.
whether he will know. the sudden widening.

*

five petals. three below. two above. a fluted corolla. spurred.
difficult to press. it is not possible to see the whole

without cutting. and this would make it into something else.
the listener must infer what cannot be said.

here, the plantsman uses profile to create an expression
of hope. but you cannot see the white inner tongue, or the purple lines

that invite you in. only the spur.
only the color that comes just before night to the edge of the fields.

*

at her breast he sees. the dream again.
the same gray, violet light. the look on her face. watching him watching her.

how he brings her to his tongue. can she feel herself pressed against his teeth? the fullness
of her skin inside his mouth? can he know what she feels? can she know what he sees?

this sacred, secret line—what passes in between? is it a gift? is it a promise?
tell me what you see. tell me what you feel.

the artemisia

*

she is spinning at the yellow leaves. the sills. again.
petals open to the light. paper thin. translucent.
at dusk, the colors of the shadows inside the grass
deepen and I see. finally. the flowers. that were there before. already.
naming themselves again for me.

cottonwood

at night, in the rain
the forest's a room full of books.

a chorus of trees!
yes, but there's a place I need to make, still.

I wanted to live on the mesa. grow a garden.
I thought it would be enough. *a table? a painted chair?*

and a blue-square view of the sky. cottonwood in it.
it's like a map of the country you never leave.

where the water rises out of the corners of rock
and the ditch-bank's sewn together by roots.

you can see where the weaving begins. you're willow-bound.
          —it's the leaning I love.

—*like an invitation?* yes. right here. where the road dumps you out in the middle
of no-place. and you walk. toward something. straight across the bare curve of it.

and the wind in everything. —look what they do to the sky. *the vaulted arches. the secret rooms.*
all the places I have lived. the windows. and the rain. and the leaves.

and look what happens to possibility, the imagination of a life: a stem branching out
from the slightest breeze becomes a limb. becomes a tree. —something it never thought.

—*and yet it stays. here.* —not on the mesa. but down below, in the crevices of rock.
where the water comes. that choice.

—*thirst?* —yes.

          and so.

                    once upon a time...
          they found themselves again. —*side by side.*

                    in the deepest shade.

                              by the waters, most perfect.

exactitude

what is drawn out from within
precisely—*as honeysuckle*—yes!

what is nurtured there—*long
white filament, slowly plucked.*

as in: this single, evanescent,
glance.

it is a sip. sidelong. sunfall.

and the burnished green beneath.
ovate-smooth. net-veined.

as in night-comes-gleaming—yes,
the sea its jeweled breast, this

leaning into—*arms wide, into.
and taste!*—nothing but a starlit wooden boat.

mixed conifer

it's a city made of fabric and rock.
a marketplace of color, incendiary...

as wind in the pines.
and the little elk sedge.

—we're traveling together on busses and trains
clattering through traffic, gesticulating

and the gauzy dust that clings to the duff after the snow leaves.
and the muted shades of lichen. stems of grass twining upward, scripted, inside

—till you reach across the bank of seats, climb over—
and onto me. pinning me to the ground. pressing me down.

needle-cast, twinned. limber and white fir and spruce and ponderosa, glistening
their webby lines and the wind in everything

and my hands at your waist
and your hair streaming down

and my fingers and arms, silvers and greens and golds
and I'm looking up at you, and our eyes meet, just once—parsing and pouring and given—

not letting go.

in the beginning, in these same woods, before I knew anything, you turned to wait for me.
here. in this place. you were laughing and leaving, both, at once, in waves—

—*look! come quick*—
every doorway is gleaming!

la vita nuova

years pass.
some a little harder than the rest.
sedges fill my dreams. my garden.

some things are certain.
half the color of winter. half the color of wheat.
the warmth that rises in between.

our roots gather into nets.
little cups of earth. eyes lifted.
always. the smallest, sweetest song.

coda: a manuscript of letters

pinaceae   *salicaceae*   *rosaceae*

cyperaceae   *poaceae*   *iridaceae*

primulaceae   *onagraceae*   *campanulaceae*

malvaceae   *solanaceae*   *violaceae*

fabaceae   *liliaceae*   *orchidaceae*

*   *   *

winter	water	wind
once	to grace	the wren
the night	a song	to lift
to know	upon	the sky
rooting	rising	rain
to stay	to leaf	to keep
oh still	oh flame	oh swift
behold	to leap	the light
oh mine	oh glance	oh friend
oh bright	increase	the flute
awake	to earth	to dream
the speak	the sweet	the moon
of wound	of air	a voice
from dawn	from noon	from dusk
to ache	to see	to cross
the dark	within	the wing
conjure	the lace	my love
the thread	to knit	the lark
to mend	this now	with you
my heart	to dwell	to stay

NOTES

"Let us begin again." Roland Barthes, *A Lover's Discourse*, Hill and Wang, New York, 1977, p. 24. [Italics in original].

"She was the wind…" Theodore Roethke, "The Vigil," in *Collected Poems,* Anchor Books, Doubleday, 1975 edition, p. 103.

"Originally, Artemis was ruler of the stars." Robert Graves, *The Greek Myths*, Penguin Books, London, England, 1992. n. 4, p. 86.

"—at this point, she is all bird." Anne Baring and Jules Cashford, *The Myth of the Goddess*, Arkana, Penguin Group, London, England, 1991. p. 322, citing Jane Ellen Harrison, *Themis, a study of the social origins of Greek religion*, Cambridge University Press, New York, 1927, p. 114.

THE ARTEMISIA

Artemis is the Archeress, hunter, goddess of forests and hills, Apollo's twin sister, and guardian of girls, wild animals and wilderness.

-ia. Suffix, used to form abstract nouns of feminine gender. Derived from or pertaining to countries, maladies, flowers, or rarely collections of things.

Artemisia: any of a genus of aromatic composite herbs and shrubs favored by Artemis. Wormwood, mugwort, tarragon, absinthe, sage.

Pinaceae (pine), Salicaceae (willow), Rosaceae (rose), Cyperaceae (sedge), Poaceae (grass), Iridaceae (iris), Primulaceae (primrose), Onagraceae (evening primrose), Campanulaceae (harebell), Malvaceae (mallow), Solanaceae (nightshade), Violaceae (violet), Fabaceae (legume), Liliaceae (lily), Orchidaceae (orchid). These are some of the wild native plant families that may be found in or along the edges of high mountain meadows, wetlands and streams in the Rocky Mountain west.

"the shape of an unknown thing." Michael Ondaatje, *Running in the Family*, First Vintage International Edition, 1982, p. 190.

I

"And within the deepest shade/the innermost recess, there lay a cave/most perfect." From Ovid, *The Metamorphoses, Book III, Actaeon.* Translated by Allen Mandelbaum. Everyman's Library, Alfred A. Knopf, 2013. p. 84.

In Section I, all the language in italics, the second voice, is drawn directly from the personal letters and correspondence of my friend Greta Nelson. Borrowed with her gracious permission.

THE HISTORY OF A COLOR:

The title is taken from Green: The History of a Color, by Michel Pastoureau, Princeton University Press, 2014. In ancient Greek, there were no words for what we think of today as the color green. Homer used the word "glaukos" to describe the color of water, the color of eyes, the color of leaves, and the color of honey. Pastoureau writes that the Greek word "glaukos" "conveys the idea of a color's paleness or weak concentration rather than a precisely defined shade." The first words in any western lexicon denoting what we think of today as the chromatic hues of green arose in Latin during Roman times. Pastoureau, p. 20.

"Viridis," "viridine," "viridescence," "verdance," "verdure," and "verdet" mean green, or pertain to various shades of green and derive from the Latin verb "vireo" to green.

For Goethe, darkness was not an absence of light, but rather, a polarity of lightness like the poles of a magnet, which interacted with light; color resulted from this interaction of light and shadow. "Yellow is a light which has been dampened by darkness; Blue is a darkness weakened by light." Goethe, Johann, *Theory of Colours*, 1810. paragraph #502. For Goethe, green is the color that arises when light and darkness interact equally.

INK:

This poem alludes to several lines from Marie Howe's poem "The Girl at 3" in *Magdalene*, W.W. Norton & Co., 2017, p. 56. "(The book I'm reading says that what we have to do,/ within ourselves, to learn to read--creates a self,/but when we've created that self we've created an edge/that separates us from the world we long for/:the interiority we create by reading is rich and lonely.)"

LA GRÂCE D'UN VOL:

The title and "comme elles tombent bien!" are from *Cyrano de Bergerac*, by Edmond Rostand, Act V, scene v. Cyrano describing the falling leaves to Roxanne: "Comme elles tombent bien!/Dans ce trajet si court de la branche à la terre,/Comme elles savent mettre une beauté dernière,/Et malgré leur terreur de pourrir sur le sol,/Veulent que cette chute ait la grâce d'un vol!" My poor translation: How perfectly they fall!/In this short distance from branch to earth,/How they know to trace a last beauty,/And in spite of their fear of perishing on the ground,/Long for this descent to have the grace of flight!

Also, the phrase "simple rain" refers to "how shy the attraction of simple rain" the opening line from the poem "Water Table" by James Galvin. *God's Mistress*, Harper and Row Publishers, NY, 1984.

BEGINNING, FRAGMENTS:

This poem alludes to three fragments of Emily Dickinson's Third 'Master Letter'. See, *The Master Letters of Emily Dickinson*, ed. R. W. Franklin, Amherst College Press, 1986, p. 35, 39.

"- I did'nt
tell you for a long time - but
I knew you had altered me-"

"I am older - tonight, Master -
but the love is the same -
so are the moon and the
crescent-"

"- and did the
sea - ever come so close as
to make you dance?"

Also, "like wind and flame upward together" is from Rumi in *The Soul of Rumi, A New Collection of Ecstatic Poems*, translated by Coleman Barks, Harper Collins, New York, NY, 2001, p. 350.

Also, "I am broken with longing." Sappho fragment 102; translated by Anne Carson. *If Not, Winter, Fragments of Sappho*. Vintage Books, New York, 2002. p. 203.

Also, "My ears have yet not drunk a hundred words/Of thy tongue's uttering, yet I know the sound." Juliet. William Shakespeare, *Romeo and Juliet*, Act II, scene ii, lines 58-59.

THE LAKE, ONLY WATER:

"only water" refers to a line in Ted Hughes' "Actaeon" in *Tales From Ovid*, Farrar Straus and Giroux, New York, 1997, p. 99: "No weapon was to hand—only water."

SUBTEXT:

"songlines" is an allusion to *The Songlines* by Bruce Chatwin, Penguin Books, 1987.

"as a picture of things" refers to Simonides' philosophy of art and especially the referential quality of the language of poetry: "The word of things a picture is," as translated and discussed in *Economy of the Unlost* by Anne Carson, Princeton University Press, 1999, p. 46-52.

"in the sweetapple tree" is a reference to Sappho fragment 105A. See note for "the sweetapple tree" below.

THE TEMPEST:

"The isle is full of noises" Caliban. William Shakespeare, *The Tempest*, Act III, scene ii, line 144.

"I don't know what to do/two states of mind in me" Sappho, fragment 51; translated by Anne Carson. *If Not, Winter, Fragments of Sappho*. Vintage Books, New York, 2002. p. 107.

"and this to me—/the brilliance and beauty of the sun—desire has allotted" Sappho fragment 58; translated by Anne Carson. *If Not, Winter, Fragments of Sappho*. Vintage Books, New York, 2002. p. 121.

THE SWEETAPPLE TREE:

This poem alludes to Sappho fragment 105A: "as the sweetapple reddens on a high branch/ high on the highest branch and the applepickers forgot—/no, not forgot: were unable to reach" Translated by Anne Carson. *If Not, Winter, Fragments of Sappho*. Vintage Books, New York, 2002. p. 215. See also, Carson's enlightening commentary: "the poem begins in a simile which has no *comparandum*, and a relative clause which never reaches completion in a main verb...if there is a bride here, she remains inaccessible; it is her inaccessibility that is present, grammatically and erotically. Desiring hands close upon empty air in the final infinitive." p. 373-374.

Also, in Ovid's account of the story of Artemis and Actaeon, after she casts water on the hunter, Artemis says: "Now go, feel free to say that you have seen the goddess without veils—if you can speak." Ovid, *The Metamorphoses, Book III.* Translated by Allen Mandelbaum. Everyman's Library, Alfred A. Knopf, 2013. p. 85.

II

"Artemis half revealed caught up her dress and encircling shawl, and sank with gliding limbs into the water, until by little and little all her form was hidden." from Nonnos, *Dionysiaca, V,* translated by W. H. D. Rouse, Harvard University Press, Cambridge, MA, 1940, p. 191.

"The branches that he parted to get a better view/now grew in the place of eyes" from Norman O. Brown, *Apocalypse and/or Metamorphosis*, University of California Press, Berkeley and Los Angeles, CA, 1991, p. 40.

"Do we get another life?   *Oh yes./Maybe not in this place.   Maybe in different forms.*" from "Diana" by Jean Valentine, *Break the Glass*, Copper Canyon Press, Port Townsend, WA, 2010, p. 50. [Italics in original].

THE MIRRORS OF ACTAEON

(A WINTER CONSTELLATION):

In some tellings, Orion the hunter was said to be the only mortal man that Artemis ever loved. Apollo was not pleased. One morning as Orion was swimming in the sea, Apollo tricked his sister by challenging her to a shooting contest. Not knowing it was Orion, Artemis shot first at the distant swimmer and killed him. Heartbroken, she made Orion into a constellation of stars.

(IN THE HALL OF DOGS):

These are the names of some of Actaeon's dogs. Apollodorus names seven hunting dogs, (*Library* 3.4.4) while Ovid names thirty-six (*The Metamorphoses, Book III, Actaeon)*, and Hyginus names eighty-two dogs (*Fabulae* 181).

(BY THE WATERS):

These are three river-bank sedges: *Carex aquatilis, pellita and utriculata*: water sedge, woolly sedge and beaked sedge.

(APRIL'S CASEMENT):

In Greek mythology, Chiron was the Centaur who trained Actaeon to be a hunter. After Actaeon's death, the dogs, ignorant of what they had done, came to the cave of Chiron seeking their master. The Centaur fashioned an image of Actaeon in order to soothe their grief.

THE CAUSES OF DECAY:

The title is drawn from hexagram 18, "recognizing and correcting the causes of decay" from the I Ching, *The Oracle of the Cosmic Way*, as translated and interpreted by Carol K. Anthony and Hanna Moog, ICHINGBOOKS, Stow, MA, 2002, p. 185. This hexagram describes the process of identifying the collective beliefs that interfere with one's ability to follow his or her own unique truth.

The end of this poem is an homage to "Natalia" by Ilya Kaminsky in *Dancing in Odessa*, Tupelo Press, 2004.

III

"Still to this day, some evenings I hear a voice calling me by name in the street. A somewhat husky voice. It drags a bit around certain syllables, and I recognize it immediately. I turn around but there's nobody there. Not only in the evenings but during that sluggish part of those summer afternoons when you're no longer even sure what year it is. All will be as it was before./I often hear that voice in my dreams." Patrick Modiano, *In the Café of Lost Youth*, translated from the French by Chris Clarke, New York Review of Books, NY, 2007. p. 85.

"She came without sound,/Without brushing the wet stones,/In the soft dark of early evening,/She came,/The wind in her hair,/The moon beginning." Theodore Roethke, "The Visitant," in *Collected Poems*, Anchor Books, Doubleday, 1975 edition, p. 96.

THE LEAST WAVE:

The title is drawn from Theodore Roethke's poem "Bring the Day!" "I've listened into the least waves./The grass says what the wind says:/Begin with the rock;/End with water." in *Collected Poems*, Anchor Books, Doubleday, 1975 edition, p. 73.

CALYPSO:

This is an ekphrastic poem based on a photograph of the Great Sand Dunes at dawn by Taos photographer, Elizabeth Burns. In Greek mythology, Calypso was a nymph who lived alone on an island and who, after rescuing Odysseus, fell in love, nursed him back to health, gave birth to their two children, and offered to be his partner for eternity, if he would only stay with her. After seven years, under pressure from Zeus and Athena, and faced with Odysseus' inexplicable lack of enthusiasm, she let him go, but not without providing a raft, wine, food and wind for the rest of his journey home.

THE VEILS (*VIOLA ADUNCA*):

Viola adunca is a species of wild violet known as hookedspur, or early blue violet.

"there is a sacred, secret line in loving" from an untitled poem in *Twenty Poems*, Anna Akhamatova, translated by Jane Kenyon, Nineties Press & Ally Press, St. Paul, Minnesota, 1985, p. 17.

COTTONWOOD:

"the deepest shade" and "most perfect" are from Ovid: "And within the deepest shade/ the innermost recess, there lay a cave/most perfect." *The Metamorphoses, Book III, Actaeon.* Translated by Allen Mandelbaum. Everyman's Library, Alfred A. Knopf, 2013. p. 84.

EXACTITUDE:

"exactitude" is one of Italo Calvino's essays in *Six Memos for the Next Millennium*, Houghton Mifflin Harcourt, NY, 1988, p. 67. Calvino writes: "Words connect the visible track to the invisible thing, the absent thing, the thing that is desired or feared, like a fragile makeshift bridge cast across the void." p. 94.

LA VITA NUOVA:

After the *Mottetti, Poems of Love* by Eugenio Montale, as translated by Dana Gioia, Graywolf Press, St. Paul MN, 1999. And of course, Dante.

ABOUT THE AUTHOR

William S. Barnes is the author of two books of poetry: *The Ledgerbook* (3:A Taos Press, 2016) and *the artemisia* (Inlandia Institute, 2024) national winner of the 2022 Hillary Gravendyk Prize for Poetry. Poems from *the artemisia* have appeared in *Comstock, Crab Creek, Mudfish, Oberon*, and *Ocotillo Reviews* and the *Taos Journal of Poetry*, among others. He is a botanist, former attorney, former middle school science and language arts teacher, and currently works as an ecologist for the New Mexico State Land Office. He lives in Santa Fe. http://williamsbarnes.com

ACKNOWLEDGMENTS

Grateful acknowledgment to the editors of the following publications in which some of these poems have previously appeared, sometimes in slightly altered form.

Bangalore Review: "subtext"
Comstock Review: "the lake, only water" (Special Merit, 2022 Muriel Craft Bailey Memorial Award)
Crab Creek Review: "la grace d'un vol" (Semi-finalist, 2022 Crab Creek Review Poetry Prize)
Ilanot Review: "beginning, fragments" "exactitude"
Musings: "postcard, artemisia"
Mudfish Review: "ink" "the veils (*viola adunca*)" (2nd Honorable Mention, 2021 Mudfish Poetry Prize)
Oberon Poetry Magazine: "deciduous" (Winner, 2022 Oberon Herbert Poetry Prize)
Ocotillo Review: "severance" (Winner, 2021 Julia Darling Memorial Prize)
Sixfold Review: "the history of a color" "to hatch" "the waters" "the least wave"
Taos Journal of Poetry: "calypso" "cottonwood"
Tupelo Press, The Last Milkweed Anthology: "the art of collage"

I am so grateful to the Inlandia Institute, Inlandia Books, Cati Porter, Maria Fernanda Vidaurrazaga, and especially the judges Stacey Callies, Charles Legere and Megan Gravendyk-Estrella for selecting this work. I am deeply honored to be associated with Hillary Gravendyk whose poems are an astonishment. Also, special thanks to Laurie Kaplowitz for permission to use her beautiful painting *Maidenhair Tree* for the cover.

I am indebted to the faculty at NYU Paris. Abundant gratitude to the keepers of the Solarium at the Mabel Dodge Luhan House in Taos, and to all the writers and artists at La Muse Inn in Labastide-Esparbairenque, France. I am indebted to my colleagues at the New Mexico State Land Office for letting me go again and again. I am forever grateful to my friend Nadine Karel, for orchestrating all the adventures, and for always returning.

Also, this book could not have happened without the companionship of the brilliant community of poets in Taos and Santa Fe, especially Gary Worth Moody, Cathy Strisik, Sawnie Morris, Katherine DeSeluja, Tina Carlson and Stella Reed. Special thanks to Lise Goett for her inciteful edits and the deepest gratitude to Veronica Golos whose friendship and support, and help reading and re-reading these poems has been invaluable.

And thank you dearest family: Julia, Mikaela, Craig, Eli, Jennifer, Noelle, Brian, Michael, Nathan and Cody for your love and inspiration. Especially, thank you Julia for supporting me in so many ways and making everything possible.

Finally, the idea for this story, and the correspondence that hatched it into being, belong to my friend Greta Nelson—seamstress, meadowlark, soulfriend—brilliant canopy of leaves. Sometimes life brings more love than you know how to hold. And you have to ask, like the song, *Why me? How'd I get this Hallelujah?* And there's no answer. Just a smile, a nod. And then she turns and leaves. And you know she has to go. And you know, somehow, your life's been changed forever. *There's no going back.* But a song in your pocket. And love. *And a wildness unbound.*

PERMISSIONS

Anna Akhmatova, excerpt from untitled poem in Twenty Poems, Anna Akhmatova, translated by Jane Kenyon, from Collected Poems of Jane Kenyon. Copyright © 2005 by The Estate of Jane Kenyon. Reprinted with the permission of The Permissions Company, LLC on behalf of Graywolf Press, graywolfpress.org.

Eugenio Montale, after Mottetti, Poems of Love: The Motets of Eugenio Montale, translated by Dana Gioia (St. Paul, Minnesota: Graywolf Press, 1990). Copyright © 1990 by Dana Gioia. Reprinted with the permission of the translator.

Ovid, excerpts from Book III, The Metamorphoses Of Ovid: A New Verse Translation by Allen Mandelbaum. Copyright © 1993 by Allen Mandelbaum. Used by permission of HarperCollins Publishers.

Theodore Roethke, excerpts from "The Vigil" and "The Visitant" from The Collected Poems of Theodore Roethke. Copyright 1950 by Theodore Roethke. Copyright © 1966 by Beatrice Roethke, Administratrix of the Estate of Theodore Roethke. Used by permission of Doubleday, an imprint of the Knopf Doubleday Publishing Group, a division of Penguin Random House LLC. All rights reserved.

Sappho, Fragment 51 and excerpt from Fragment 58, translated by Anne Carson from If Not, Winter: Fragments of Sappho. Copyright © 2002 by Anne Carson. Used by permission of Alfred A. Knopf, an imprint of the Knopf Doubleday Publishing Group, a division of Penguin Random House LLC. All rights reserved.

Jean Valentine, excerpt from "Diana" from Break the Glass. Copyright © 2010 by Jean Valentine. Reprinted with the permission of The Permissions Company, LLC on behalf of Copper Canyon Press, coppercanyonpress.org.

ABOUT THE HILLARY GRAVENDYK PRIZE

The Hillary Gravendyk Prize is an open poetry book competition published by Inlandia Institute for all writers regardless of the number of previously published poetry collections.

HILLARY GRAVENDYK (1979-2014) was a beloved poet living and teaching in Southern California's "Inland Empire" region. She wrote the acclaimed poetry book, *HARM* from Omnidawn Publishing (2012) and the posthumoussly published *The Soluble Hour* (Omnidawn, 2017) and *Unlikely Conditions* (1913 Press, 2017, with Cynthia Arrieu-King) as well as the poetry chapbook *The Naturalist* (Anchiote Press, 2008). A native of Washington State, she was an admired Assistant Professor of English at Pomona College in Claremont, CA. Her poetry has appeared widely in journals such as *American Letters & Commentary, The Bellingham Review, The Colorado Review, The Eleventh Muse, Fourteen Hills, MARY, 1913: A Journal of Forms, Octopus Magazine, Tarpaulin Sky and Sugar House Review*. She was awarded a 2015 Pushcart Prize for her poem "Your Ghost," which appeared in the Pushcart Prize Anthology. She leaves behind many devoted colleagues, friends, family and beautiful poems. Hillary Gravendyk passed away on May 10, 2014 after a long illness. This contest has been established in her memory.

ABOUT INLANDIA INSTITUTE

Inlandia Institute is a regional non-profit and literary center. We seek to bring focus to the richness of the literary enterprise that has existed in this region for ages. The mission of the Inlandia Institute is to recognize, support, and expand literary activity in all of its forms in Inland Southern California by publishing books and sponsoring programs that deepen people's awareness, understanding, and appreciation of this unique, complex and creatively vibrant region.

The Institute publishes books, presents free public literary and cultural programming, provides in-school and after school enrichment programs for children and youth, holds free creative writing workshops for teens and adults, and boot camp intensives. In addition, every two years, the Inlandia Institute appoints a distinguished jury panel from outside of the region to name an Inlandia Literary Laureate who serves as an ambassador for the Inlandia Institute, promoting literature, creative literacy, and community. Laureates to date include Susan Straight (2010-2012), Gayle Brandeis (2012-2014), Juan Delgado (2014-2016), Nikia Chaney (2016-2018), and Rachelle Cruz (2018-2020).

To learn more about the Inlandia Institute, please visit our website at www.InlandiaInstitute.org.

OTHER HILLARY GRAVENDYK PRIZE BOOKS

Bones Awaiting The Blaze by Tiffany Elliott
Winner of the 2022 Regional Hillary Gravendyk Prize

How To Know You're Dreaming When You're Dreaming, Lesson One
   by Angelica Maria Barraza Tran
Winner of the 2021 National Hillary Gravendyk Prize

Our Lady of Perpetual Desert by Alexandra Martinez
Winner of the 2021 Regional Hillary Gravendyk Prize

among the enemies by Michael Samra
Winner of the 2020 National Hillary Gravendyk Prize

This Side of the Fire by Jonathan Maule
Winner of the 2020 Regional Hillary Gravendyk Prize

The Silk the Moths Ignore by Bronwen Tate
Winner of the 2019 National Hillary Gravendyk Prize

Remyth: A Postmodern Ritual by Adam D. Martinez
Winner of the 2019 Regional Hillary Gravendyk Prize

Former Possessions of the Spanish Empire by Michelle Peñaloza
Winner of the 2018 National Hillary Gravendyk Prize

All the Emergency-Type Structures by Elizabeth Cantwell
Winner of the 2018 Regional Hillary Gravendyk Prize

Our Bruises Kept Singing Purple by Malcolm Friend
Winner of the 2017 National Hillary Gravendyk Prize

Traces of a Fifth Column by Marco Maisto
Winner of the 2016 National Hillary Gravendyk Prize

God's Will for Monsters by Rachelle Cruz
Winner of the 2016 Regional Hillary Gravendyk Prize
Winner of a 2018 American Book Award

Map of an Onion by Kenji C. Liu
Winner of the 2015 National Hillary Gravendyk Prize

All Things Lose Thousands of Times by Angela Peñaredondo
Winner of the 2015 Regional Hillary Gravendyk Prize

www.ingramcontent.com/pod-product-compliance
Lightning Source LLC
Chambersburg PA
CBHW081410270326
41931CB00016B/3434

9 781955 969253